Mel Bay Presents

AMERICAN TREASURES

Early American Ballads, Hymns, & Songs of Patriotism

For Solo Guitar
by Phillip Lester
&
Transcribed by Bill Piburn

D1716034

Online audio

Cover Painting by Paul Chase

To Access the Online Audio Go To:
www.melbay.com/20045BCDEB

1 2 3 4 5 6 7 8 9 0

Visit us on the Web at www.melbay.com — E-mail us at email@melbay.com

Endorsements of American Treasures

"With creative, mezmerizing arrangements, Phillip Lester has once again combined technical ability and the artistry of the guitar to bring us the true essence of these songs. Each arrangement brings out the deep beauty of songs that helped to shape our country and helps us to understand how they have remained in the American consciousness through times of deep patriotism as well as times of apathy and protest.... American Treasures is a definitve collection of the songs that have become an essential part of the fabric of our flag and of this great country of ours."

— E. Sherwin Mackintosh

"The arrangements are superb, as is the playing. We especially like the military sound of "Chester," old William Billings would have loved it: you've caught the spirit in which he wrote it! Thanks again".

— Sam Hinton - La Jolla, CA

"..one of the nicest guitar albums I've ever heard. You honor these great melodies with sensitive, soulful playing."

— guitarist, El McMeen,
www.elmcmeen.com

"I listened to your entire CD last week. I liked the overall sense of reverence for the music. I liked your guitar sound throughout. I liked the selections themselves and the playing order seems to be paced well. I'm glad that you stuck to solo guitar for this too [it would have been an easy decision to add snare drum or fife to a revolutionary war tune or banjo to a Steven Foster tune, etc.]. The haunting quality of just guitar is nice. I like your slight variances in melody and the elongating of certain phrases. You did just enough of this to put your own signature to these pieces without going too far and wrecking them - a tasteful display. The same is true for chordal harmonies - just enough variance to make the pieces fresh to the ear, sometimes haunting, but not too much so as to rewrite them. I caught your little 'Chet' thumbpicking on the one tune. It's cool because it alludes to that style, but due to the nylon string sound and the lack of a thumb pick, it still sounds classical too. Your drum effects were neat too. All in all, the CD is very gracious and listenable, and I think, quite publishable as a book collection as well.
Congratulations on getting this huge project completed!
- it's a very good CD!"

— John Standefer - Vancouver, WA

Phillip Lester's "American Treasures" is a lovely collection of early American music for classical guitar. These are sensitive, thoughtful arrangements for guitarists of all levels, and I congratulate Phillip on this fine publication.

— *Christopher Parkening*

Contents

American Treasures

Early American Ballads and Songs of Patriotism arranged for solo classical guitar.

Preface

These solo guitar arrangements cover a wide spectrum of American music. They include early hymns of the Pilgrims, American Revolutionary War tunes, British folk ballads that later became colonial pop songs, sea chanteys, spirituals, Civil War tunes, pioneer frontier ballads, military hymns, and songs of patriotism. They were selected for their captivating melodies and for their adaptability for solo instrumental guitar. The idea for the collection evolved over a ten-year period, beginning with an arrangement of "My Country 'Tis of Thee." I crafted this arrangement while living in Boston during the time of the Persian Gulf War, and I first performed it for commuters who took the Red Line Subway Train at Harvard in Cambridge. Yes, I was a subway musician at that time, and the response of people I met while performing encouraged me to arrange similiar patriotic favorites. These songs evoke a remembrance of the blessings of our great country and the heritage of our freedoms that we so easily take for granted.

The idea of doing this collection of memorable American tunes led me to visit dozens of libraries to better understand the history of their origins. While doing the research, I learned stories about the composers and other interesting facts, such as the popularity of the tune and how it affected a war or the political climate of its time. Getting this deeper understanding of the song played a major influence in my approach as an arranger. I attempted to reflect the spirit of the composition within each arrangement. For example, I discovered that the great tune "Chester," by William Billings, originally began as a hymn and was turned into one of the most powerful anti-British rallying songs of the American Revolution. Knowing this led me to arrange the piece as a march and to perform it with conviction.

The art of arranging songs for solo guitar can take a variety of approaches. Generally, it involves stating the theme and then finding a way to perform the melody within a harmonious chordal background and bass line simultaneously. There are several stylistic techniques and variations on the theme that can be explored as well. The guitar's polyphonic effect (the capacity to present several strands of musical lines simultaneously) is made possible by a variety of fingerstyle picking patterns and an arrangement that allows the bass and treble strings to resonate as much as possible. Accomplishing this musically requires several factors such as a fairly proficient level of playing, finding a suitable key for the song, sometimes using an alternate tuning, and keeping a lyrical style within the performance.

I wish to thank several people whose vision, encouragement, and efforts helped make this book of arrangements possible. Bill Piburn, for his work in transcribing these arrangements and for his encouragement regarding this project; Steve Rekas, for believing in the project from the beginning and for making it a priority; Mel Bay, for taking an interest in these arrangements long before the events of 9/11 and for making it possible for other guitarists to enjoy them; and John Standefer, for his musical input and friendship and for introducing me to the good people at Mel Bay.

I am especially grateful for the musical influence of Andrés Segovia, Chet Atkins, Christopher Parkening, Alex De Grassi, Tommie Jones, Sam Hinton, and Patrick Ki. The encouragement of my father and mother, Norman and Catherine Lester, and the special support of my dear friend and school colleague Vern Miller.

While all these arrangements seek to tap the rich polyphonic nature of the guitar, they are generally not that difficult or complex. I hope guitarists of all levels will enjoy these arrangements and be richly rewarded with the music that is unleashed in these great melodies. It is my privileged to offer this collection as a musical snapshot of early America and as a reminder of the amazing heritage of this great country.

Historically, in times of war and national crisis, patriotic music has played a significant role in expressing courage and building morale. At this time in our nation's history, it is my hope that this music will once again stir national pride, encourage, and comfort listeners everywhere.

— Guitarist, Phillip Lester
Glen Ridge, New Jersey

"Intelligence, patriotism…and a firm reliance on Him who has never forsaken this favored land are still competent to adjust in the best way all our present difficulty."

— *Abraham Lincoln*

Some Notes about Alternate Tunings

In regards to alternate tuning: For this project, I arranged many songs in the key of G, and therefore it became useful to tune down the 5th string to a G. Playing the fifth string open allows for much more resonance in the bass and provides a strong musical backdrop (in two octaves) on which to play the melody. Tuning down the 6th string to a D provides the same effect for songs in the key of D. Additionally, when a song is arranged in the key of G, I have found that the alternating open bass strings of D and G can sound exceptionally full and interesting when adding the melody. I have used it extensively in this collection - most noticeably in the "Stephen Foster Suite." The use of tuning down the 6th string to a C and the 5th to a G involves the same general approach and was used extensively in the "Civil War Medley." The guitar tunings on these arrangements are:

America (My Country 'Tis of Thee) DADGBE
Old Hundredth DGDGBE
Thanksgiving Prayer DGDGBE
Chester DADGBE
Greensleeves DGDGBE
Free America/Yankee Doodle DGDGBE
Johnny Has Gone for a Soldier EADGBE
Star-Spangled Banner   DGDGBE
Barbara Allen   CGDGBE
Shenandoah CADGBE
Sweet Betsy from Pike CGDGBE
Stephen Foster Suite DGDGBE
Bound for the Promised Land EADGBE
Simple Gifts DGDGBE
The Water Is Wide CGDGBE

Stories and notes about the music . . .

1. America (My Country 'Tis of Thee)

This anonymous melody first appeared in its present form in 1744 and has been used for a variety of patriotic songs including the British "God Save the King." The lyrics for "My Country 'Tis of Thee" were composed by Samuel Francis Smith after he came across the melody in a German song book that was given to him by a friend named Lowell Mason. As the story goes, Smith was impressed with the melody and composed the words in thirty minutes on a scrap of paper. He gave a copy of his lyrics along with the book back to Mason, who was also a music teacher, and who decided to teach the song to some children. On July 4, 1832, Smith was given the surprise privilege of hearing his hymn-like patriotic song performed for the first time by the children's chorus of Park Street Church in Boston.

2. Old Hundredth

This was one of the most popular hymns the pilgrims brought over on the Mayflower. It first appeared in the Genevan Psalter in 1551 with the melody credited to Louis Bourgeois. Originally the words to the hymn were based on Psalm 100. It is often sung today as "Praise God From Whom All Blessings Flow."

3. Thanksgiving Prayer

First published in 1621, this became a favorite hymn of the early Dutch settlers for Thanksgiving Day. A later version was written by Dr. Theodore Baker in 1894 entitled "We Gather Together." The joyful uplifting melody evokes a grateful heart that sets the stage for singing "Praises to His Name Who Forgets Not His Own."

4. Greensleeves

Although most of the music sung by the early pilgrims was sacred, there were a few British popular songs like Greensleeves that were also sung in the New World. This melancholy tune can be traced as far back as the time of Shakespeare. It is one of the most popular melodies of all time. The key of G minor may seem a bit unusual but was selected for the way the alternate tuning opens up some refreshing chordal voicing possibilities. The arrangement reflects the lyrics that lament "Alas, my love, you do me wrong". It some ways it could be considered an Elizabethan blues tune.

5. Chester

Beginning as a hymn, this became one of the most popular songs of the Revolutionary War. The composer, William Billings (1746-1800), is considered by many as our first significant American-born composer. He was a tanner by trade and an itinerant music teacher who also played a key role in the development of American singing schools. Several physical disabilities prevented him from fighting in the colonial army. However, being a devoted patriot, he used his musical gifts to contribute to the cause of liberty by turning his hymns into anti-British rallying songs. His music inspired the colonists in their struggle for independence. On this arrangement I have taken an approach that is reminiscent of a Renaissance lute piece in its lively melody and moving bass line. The spirit of conviction that lies within the music is even more reflected in its lyrics:

> Let tyrants shake their iron rod,
> And slavery clank her galling chains.
> We fear them not; we trust in God;
> New England's God forever reigns.
>
> When God inspired us for the fight
> Their ranks were broke, their lines were forced;
> Their ships were shattered in our sight
> Or swiftly driven from our coast.
>
> The foe comes on with haughty stride;
> Our troops advance with martial noise.
> Their veterans flee before our youth,
> And generals yield to beardless boys.
>
> What grateful offerings shall we bring?
> What shall we render to the Lord?
> Loud Hallelujahs let us sing.
> And praise His name on every chord.

Billing's lyrics demonstrate how close religion and politics were connected in early American music. Because soldiers so loved to sing this catchy tune, "Chester" became an unofficial anthem of the American Revolution.

6. Free America / Yankee Doodle

This arrangement combines "The British Grenadiers" melody with the tune we associate most with the Colonial period, "Yankee Doodle." The song was conceived by the British as an insult to the ragged appearance of the Colonial militia. Ironically, the colonists liked the tune and later used it as their theme song against the British. This arrangement blends the two melodies and seeks to recreate a uplifting colonial confidence. The arrangement incorporates the stylistic techniques of harmonics (bell chimes) and pizzicato (muted bass) for colorful effects.

7. Johnny Has Gone for a Soldier

This deeply moving folk song from the Revolutionary War period was based on an old Irish tune, "Shule Aroon," which was first sung around 1691. I selected the key of E minor for its dark and haunting qualities.

8. The Star-Spangled Banner

During the British invasion of 1812, Francis Scott Key, a young attorney, approached a British warship stationed outside Baltimore harbor to obtain the release of a friend who had been taken prisoner. Since the British naval vessel was preparing to bombard Fort McHenry, he was forced to remain on the ship and witness the attack, which lasted all night. On the morning of Sept. 13, 1814, after the clouds of smoke had cleared, Key saw the American flag still standing over the fort — a sign that the attack had failed. Moved with amazement and pride, he wrote down his feelings in a poem which he titled "The Bombardment of Fort McHenry." The search for a suitable tune to go along with his words led to the selection of a very popular tavern song, "To Anacreon in Heaven." It was officially declared our national anthem in 1931. This arrangement utilizes the resonance capabilities of the open D/G tuning.

9. Barbara Allen

This was one of the most beautiful of early American ballads brought to the New World by the early English and Scottish settlers in 1630. The song existed in many variations, and its sad story about Barbara and William was known to bring listeners to tears. Among the many renditions of this tune, my favorite one was recorded by Art Garfunkle. The theme of being "heartbroken" should be communicated when performing this piece and that's how I chose to arrange and perform it. The open C/G tuning provides the chordal background for the heartfelt melody that often switches back and forth from a lower to a higher octave.

10. Shenandoah

A chantey was a song sailors sang to help them with their work while at sea. Published in 1837, this became one of the most beloved of all chanteys. As he prepares to cross the "wide Missouri" River, the song writer tells of his love for the daughter of an Indian Chief named Shenandoah. The arrangement incorporates several tempo changes and a recurring, descending bass line to represent the feel of a flowing river. In this arrangement the 6th string is tuned to a low C. This allows the C major chordal backdrop to fill in the spaces opened up by the lingering melody notes.

11. Sweet Betsy from Pike

Western pioneers used this classic folk melody for several different songs. The tune is believed to have been based on an old English ballad. The "Sweet Betsy" version was often associated with the gold rush of the 1850's. This popular version documents the saga of a couple: Betsy and her husband, Ike, from Pike County and their troubled journey out west. Settlers often kept themselves entertained with songs like this that mixed humor with stories of courage and perseverance:

Did you ever hear tell of sweet Betsy from Pike,
Who crossed the wide prairies with her lover Ike,
With two yoke of cattle and one spotted hog,
A tall shaghai rooster, an old yaller dog?

Chorus: Sing too-ral-ioo - ral-ool-ral-I-ay,
Sing too-ral-ioo - ral-ool-ral-I-ay.

They swam the wide rivers and crossed he tall peaks,
And camped on the prairie for weeks upon weeks.
Starvation and cholera and hard work and slaughter.
They reached California spite of hell and high water.

12. The Stephen Foster Suite

This medley combines several of Foster's most beloved ballads and sentimental songs. Opening and closing with the memorable "O Susanna," the individual arrangements gently flow into each other with a gentleness that is so characteristic of Foster's music.

Stephen Foster (1826-1864) had a gift for creating beautiful melodies and for capturing the rural and romantic sentiments of America in his time. His song writing era spanned from 1845 to 1864. During that time, he composed around 200 songs. Although his songs did very well, Foster was a poor businessman and his marriage and health suffered. In 1860 he moved to New York City, where he struggled to remain creative and productive in spite of difficulties with depression, alcoholism, and tuberculosis. He died at the age of 37.

The simplicity of Foster's genius as a composer is displayed in this tapestry of familiar ballads, each one having the power to trigger nostalgic memories.

O Susanna (1846) was Foster's first successful hit song, written when he was 20. It became the theme song of the California gold rush (1849). The publisher made many thousands of dollars from it while Stephen Foster never collected a cent in royalties. Its popularity, however, motivated him to make songwriting his career.

Jeanie with the Light Brown Hair (1854), was published just after he had been reconciled with his wife, Jane. This sentimental ballad underwent a remarkable resurgence in popularity in 1941.

My Old Kentucky Home, Good Night (1852), some believe was inspired by Foster's visit to an elderly relative in Bardstown, Kentucky, where today there is a Foster museum. In 1928, this plantation melody became the state song of Kentucky.

Beautiful Dreamer was claimed as Foster's last song ever written, but evidence shows that it had been around for at least two years prior to his death. It is regarded as his finest song composed in his last years.

Old Folks at Home (1851) is probably the best-known of all of Foster's songs. It was originally composed for the Christy Minstrels who requested a ballad with the name of a river. After looking at an atlas, he found the name "Swanee," a river that runs down through Florida. In 1931, it was adopted as the state song of Florida.

13. Simple Gifts

This traditional Shaker song of worship conveyed their practice of bowing and turning. It grew in popularity following its publication in 1848 and was selected by Aaron Copeland as a central theme in his ballet masterpiece "Appalachian Spring."

14. Deep River

One of the most beautiful of all black spirituals. Like most spirituals, it expresses the yearning for a place of relief from pain and hardships. I was first introduced to this great spiritual through listening to a recording by Christopher Parkening, who performs an arrangement of Deep River by the late Timothy Howard. Although I have rearranged it with an alternate tuning, I have sought to preserve the reverence and chord changes of Howards' arrangement.

15. Bound for the Promised Land

This is an example of a Western adaptation of a folk hymn of the early pioneers. As their wagons rolled westward, they sang of their hope of finding a land they could call their own. As a hymn it goes under the title "On Jordan's Stormy Banks." The uplifting tempo reflects the optimism and courage of the spiritual and frontier pioneer. This melody was used as a recurring theme in the motion picture epic How the West Was Won.

16. The Water Is Wide

Here is another exquisite folk ballad originating from the British Isles. It was probably based on the old British love song "Waly, Waly." One of my favorite renditions of this piece is by James Taylor.

17. Fifteen Years on the Erie Canal

The song was inspired by those who spent their lives working up and down the 425 mile canal that joined Albany to Lake Erie. The canal opened in 1825 and increased the efficiency of transporting goods from the Atlantic to the West.
Here is an example of an 1800's hit song and perhaps the hippest arrangement in the collection. The arrangement stays faithful to the catchy syncopated rhythm of the song, revealing its jazzy feel. The bridge portion which ironically is about "a low bridge" jumps to using minor chords and provides a refreshing break from the main melody. The alternate tuning gives all the chords a fresh voicing in the bass line.

18. Home on the Range (Frontier Medley)

Composed in 1873, "Home on the Range" was a cowboy song about life on the open prairie. Another frontier melody, "Red River Valley," actually originated as a ballad about a region in New York state. "She'll be Coming Around the Mountain" was a tune sung by railroad workers and towns people making reference to the uncertainty of the arrival time of the next train. The arrangement for the first two tunes remains fairly straightforward, with the melody interwoven into the chordal backdrop.

The third piece begins with a moving bass line that takes a prominent role and becomes the underlying support for the melody. Harmonics are used to represent the train whistle and must be performed with precision and speed that allows the tempo to remain on track.

19. Aura Lee

W. W. Fosdick and George R. Poulton composed this tune in 1861. It became a favorite romantic song among Union soldiers and was popular in the 1880's with college glee clubs and barbershop quartets. The melody was used later by Elvis Presley in his famous song "Love Me Tender." The arrangement calls for the 5th string to be tuned down to a G while the other stings remain in standard tuning.

20. The Civil War Suite

Opening with **"Revellerie,"** the Suite moves to a serene rendition of the most popular song of that era—"Dixie's Land." Daniel Emmet composed **"Dixie"** in New York for a minstrel show in 1859. Unfortunately for Emmet, a staunch Unionist, it became the rallying tune of the Confederacy. General Pickett ordered that the song be played before the fighting started at Gettysburg. When the war ended, President Lincoln as a gesture of friendship across the lines, asked a band to play "Dixie" saying, "We have captured the Confederate army and we have also captured the Confederate tune, and both belong to us."

The Battle Cry for Freedom: 1861. George Frederick Root composed this rallying song in response to President Lincoln's appeal for more volunteers to enlist in the Union army. This shows the power of music in times of crisis. Wherever the song was performed, excitement ran high and men began rushing to enlist. Later, Lincoln himself wrote Mr. Root and thanked him for the great service he had done his country. The President said that songs of patriotism, as much as anything else, had helped in winning the Civil War.

Bonnie Blue Flag: 1861. Next to "Dixie," this was the most popular Civil War tune of the South. It was introduced in New Orleans by an English-born vaudevillian, Harry Macarthy. The tune may have originated from an old Hiberian melody, "The Irish Jaunting Car."

Lincoln and Liberty was Lincoln's campaign song using a melody based on the popular drinking song "Old Rosin the Bow."

All Quiet Along the Potomac Tonight 1861. This was a melody by John Hill Hewitt, and the lyrics were based on a poem by Ethel Lynn Beers. The song influenced both sides to prohibit snipers from shooting at pickets on guard duty.

Tenting Tonight on the Old Camp Grounds is a melancholy Civil War ballad by Walter Kitteridge. It was a song about war-weariness and longing for home. "Many are the hearts that are weary tonight, wishing for the war to cease." It is not surprising that the song was popular both in the North and in the South.

Taps was an unofficial bugle call composed by General Dan Butterfield in 1862 to help the Union army burial team. The soundtrack from the Civil War film by Ken Burns had a significant influence on my approach to this medley.

21. When Johnny Comes Marching Home

Patrick Gilmore, the famous bandmaster of the Union army, composed this in 1863 under the pseudonym Louis Lambert. Some claim the melody originated from the Irish anti-war ballad "Johnny, I Hardly Knew Ye." The song played a major role in encouraging soldiers with the hope of ending the war and returning home. Although popular with both sides, it became even more popular 35 years later during the Spanish-American War. On this arrangement I sought to keep a marching cadence in the bass while expanding on the melody. The old rock musician in me couldn't resist the opportunity to take some liberties with a middle section. One may detect some celtic influences on my variations on the theme as well. This one of my favorite arrangements to perform.

22. Armed Services Medley

The Caissons Go Rolling Along ("The Artillery Song") was composed by Edmund L. Gruber, a 1904 graduate of West Point, while a lieutenant in the Fifth Field Artillery stationed in the Philippines in 1908. It rose to popularity in the second World War. Gruber went on to become a Brigadier General. **"Wild Blue Yonder"** was originally titled "The U.S. Air Force," by its composer Robert Crawford. This song was the winner in a contest by the Air Force for a theme song in 1939. **"Anchors Aweigh,"** the Navy theme song, originated in 1906. **"From the Halls of Montezuma"** is also known as the Marine's Hymn. The melody is based on an 1867 operetta Genevieve de Brabant, by Jacques Offenbach.

23. America the Beautiful

In 1893, Katherine Lee Bates, a professor of literature at Wellesley College was teaching summer classes in Colorado Springs. After a breathtaking mountain trip up to Pikes Peak, Bates captured her thoughts in a poem. It was published on July 4, 1895. In spite of numerous attempts by composers everywhere to put her poem to their music, she favored a hymn by Samuel A. Ward called "Materna," which is the Latin word for "motherly." By 1920, Ward's tune was universally accepted as the official melody.

24. The Battle Hymn of the Republic

In 1853, William Steffe, a Southern composer of Sunday School songs wrote this tune to accompany his sermons at camp meetings. It was originally called "Brothers, Will You Meet Us?" Later the tune became popular among abolitionist groups who sang it under the title of "John Brown's Body Lies, A-moldering in His Grave." In 1861, while visiting some Union Army Camps near Maryland, Julia Ward Howe, the wife of an Army doctor, heard it being sung by Union soldiers and was moved to pen a new version. Although she was inspired to compose new lyrics, she still retained the original "Glory, Glory Hallelujah" chorus. It ultimately became the great marching song of the North and went on to be an inspirational song for movements throughout history. Upon hearing it for the first time, Abraham Lincoln was moved to tears and asked to hear it again.

This work is dedicated to all the men and women who have paid the price for freedom with their willingness to sacrifice their lives for this country.

— *Phillip Lester*

For any correspondence write to:
Phillip Lester P.O. Box 1231 Maplewood, NJ 07040
or email at GuitarArtistry@yahoo.com.

Information about performances and other recordings by guitarist Phillip Lester is available at
www.GuitarArtistry.com.

My Country 'Tis of Thee

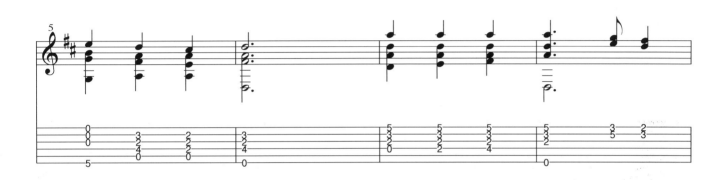

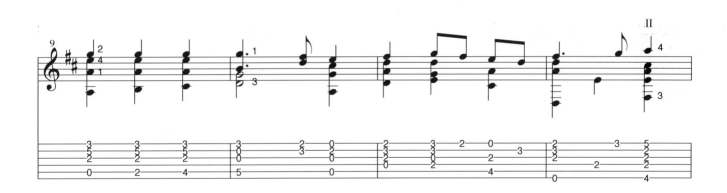

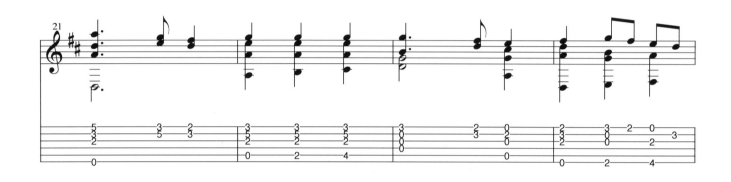

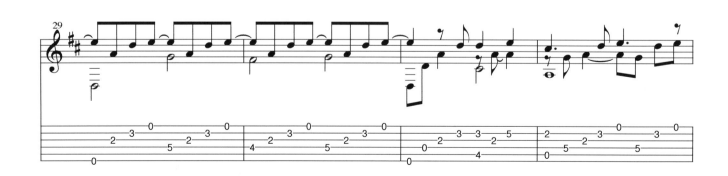

Old Hundreth

6=D
5=G

from the "Genevan Psalter"
1551

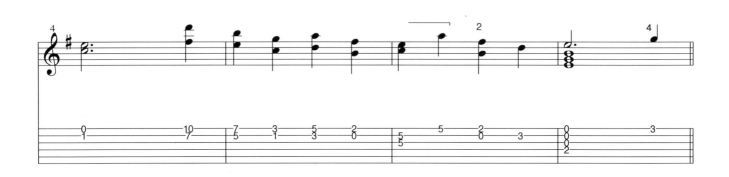

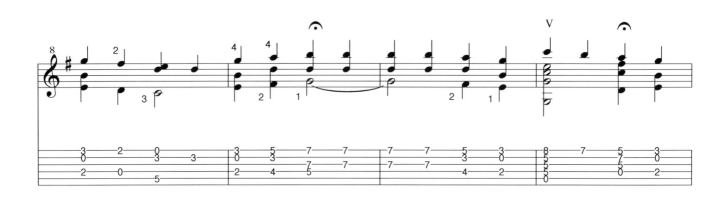

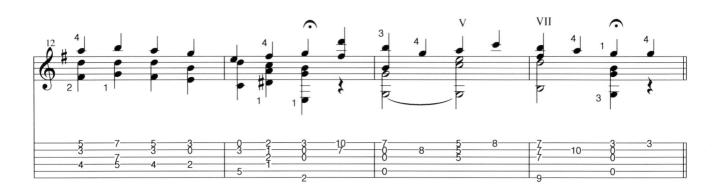

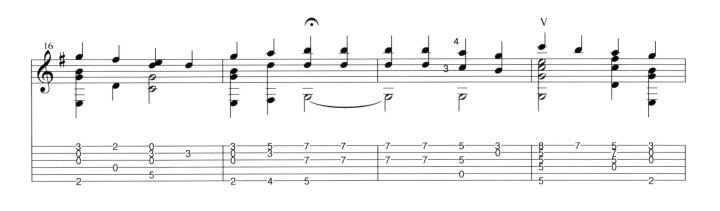

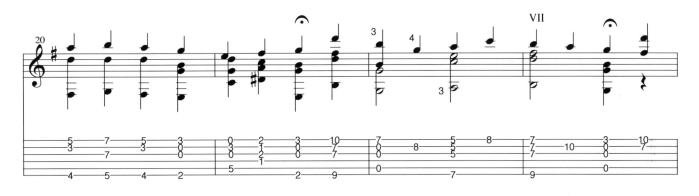

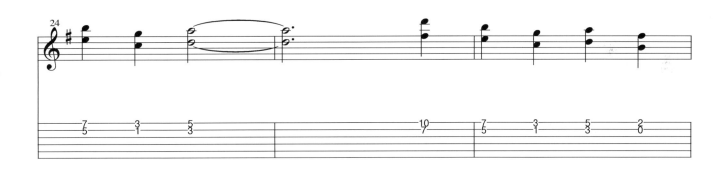

Thanksgiving Prayer

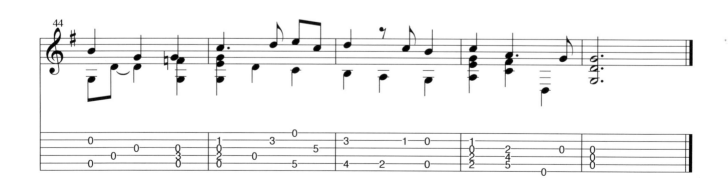

Greensleeves

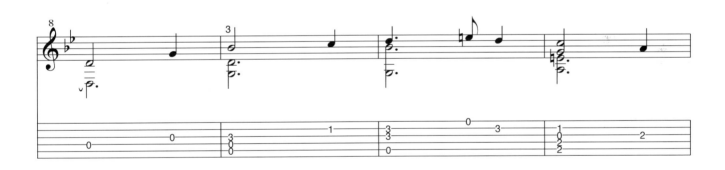

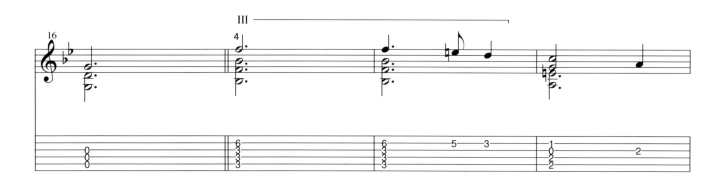

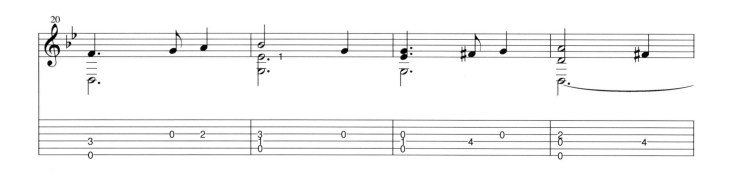

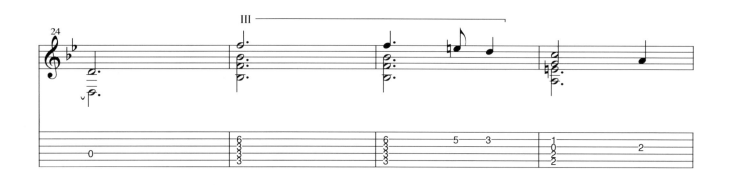

Chester

William Billings
(1746 - 1800)

6=D

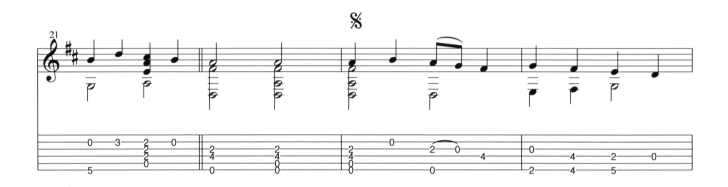

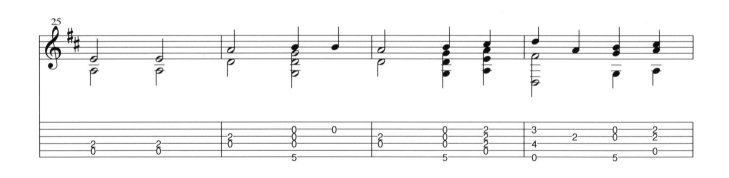

A bass 2nd time only

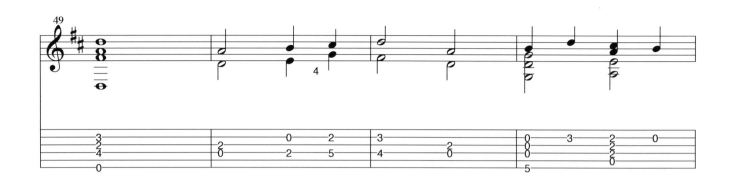

D.S. al Coda   Coda

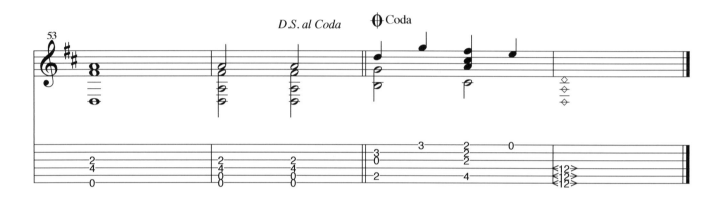

Free America/Yankee Doodle

6 = D
5 = G

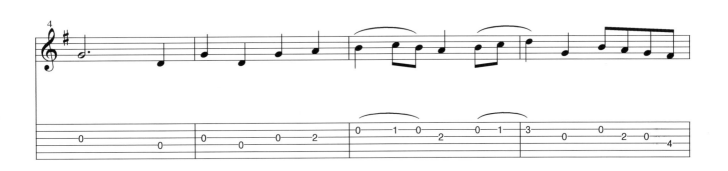

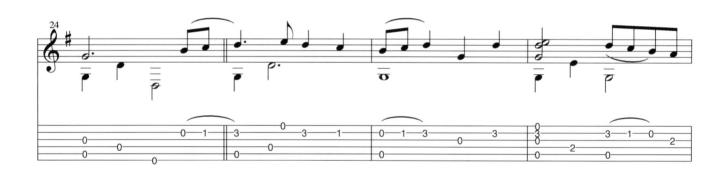

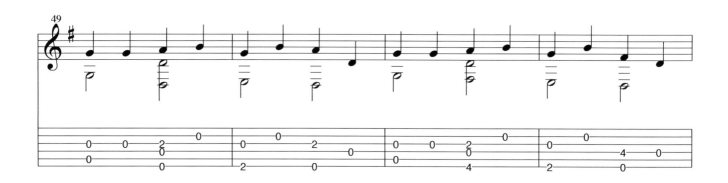

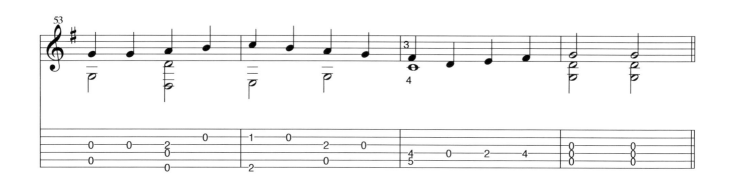

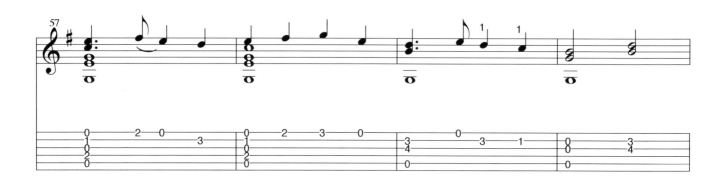

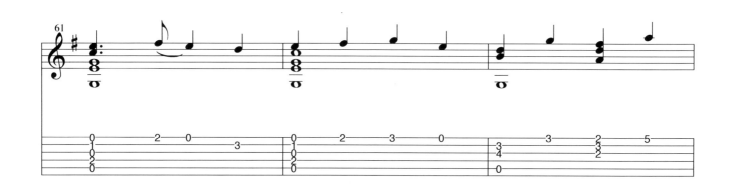

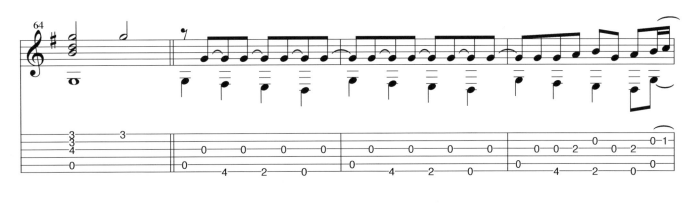

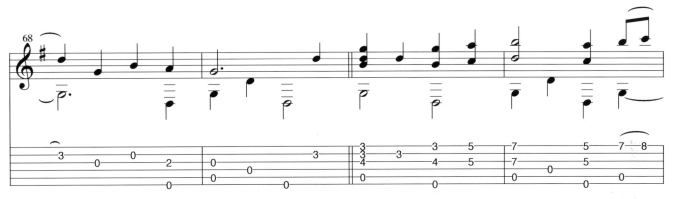

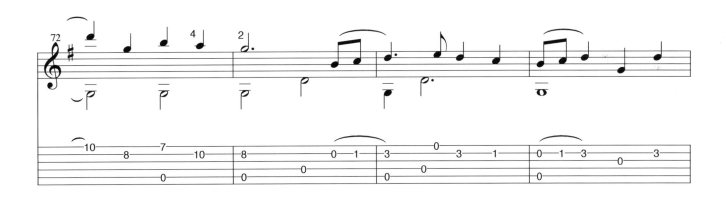

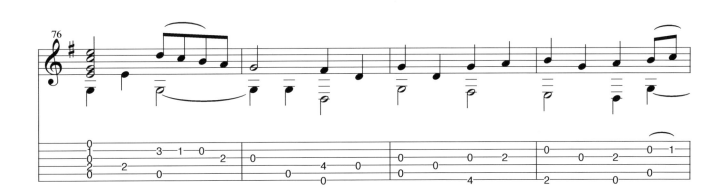

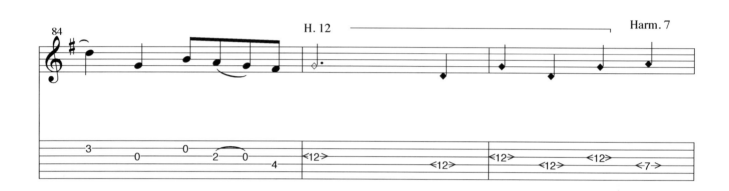

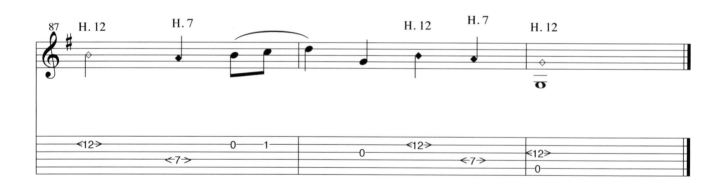

Johnny Has Gone for a Soldier

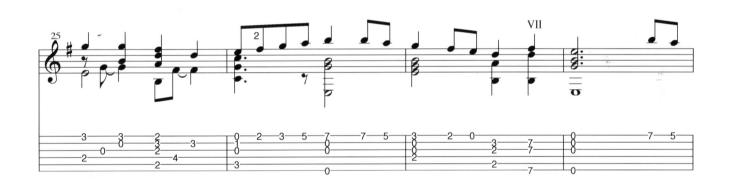

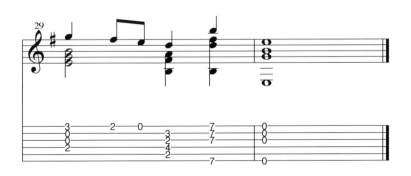

The Star-Spangled Banner

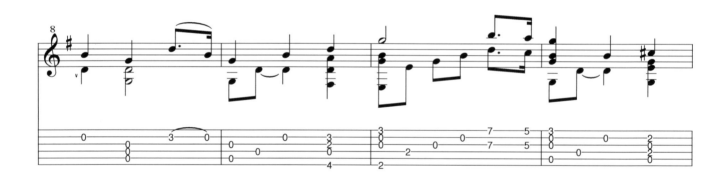

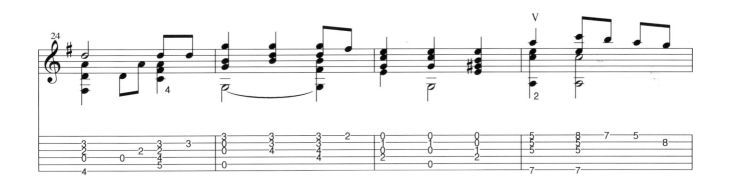

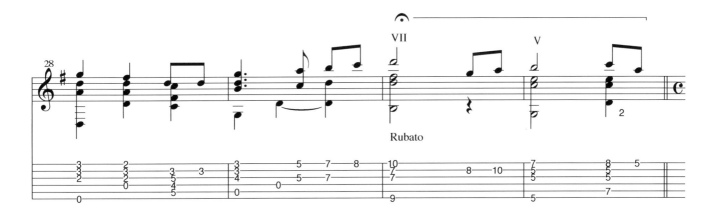

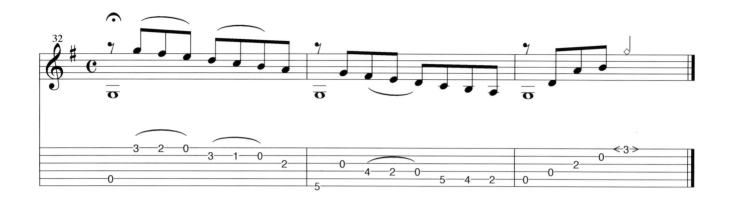

Barbara Allen

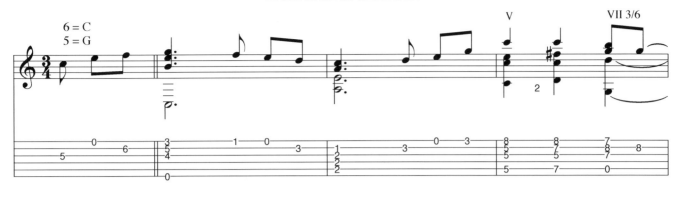

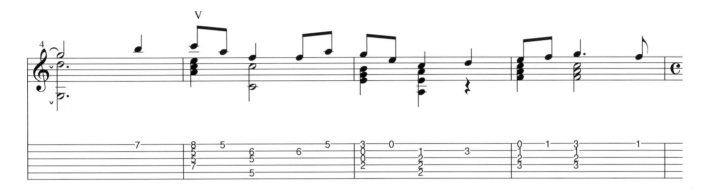

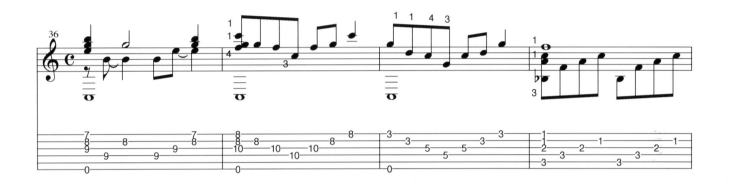

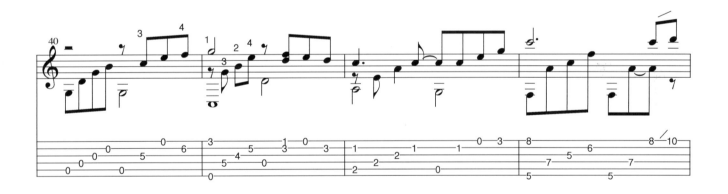

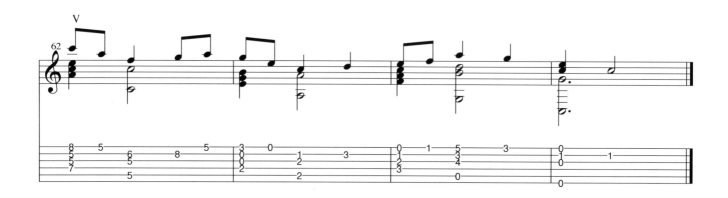

Shenandoah

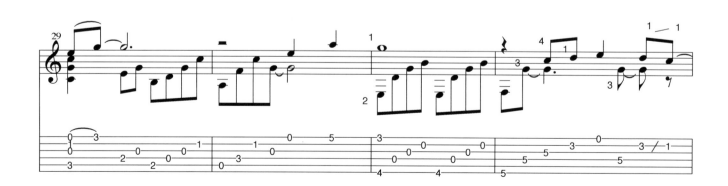

To Coda

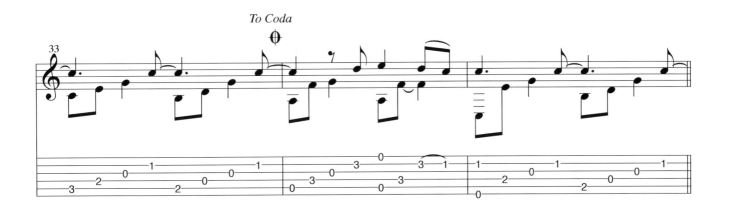

D.S. al Coda

Coda

Sweet Betsy from Pike

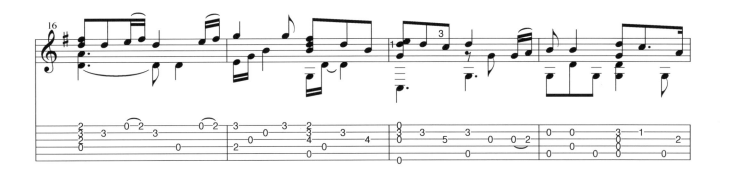

Stephen Foster Suite

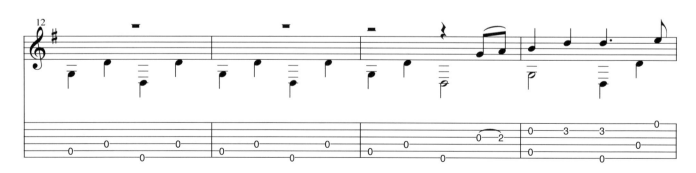

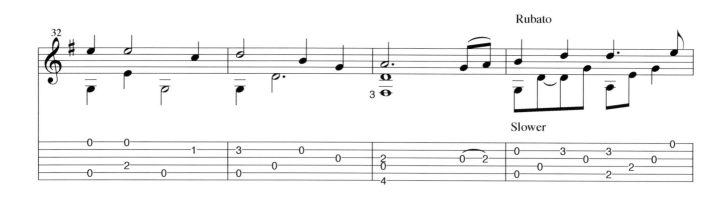

Jeanie With the Light Brown Hair

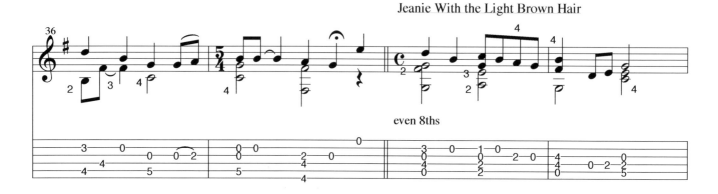

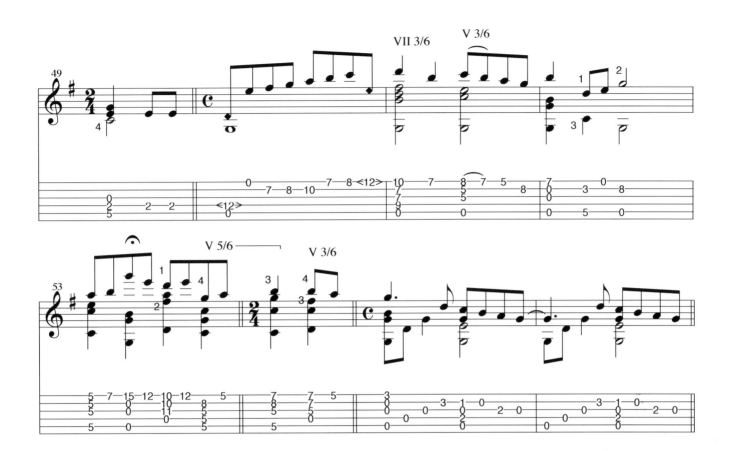

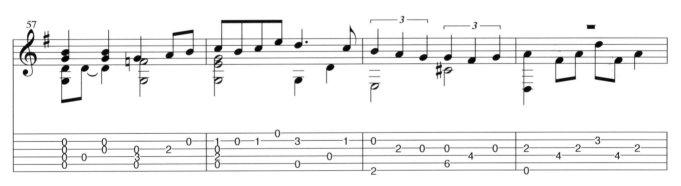

My Old Kentucky Home

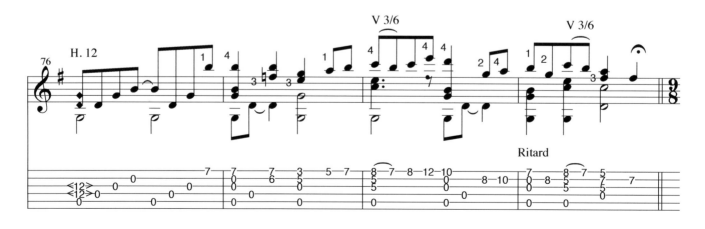

Beautiful Dreamer

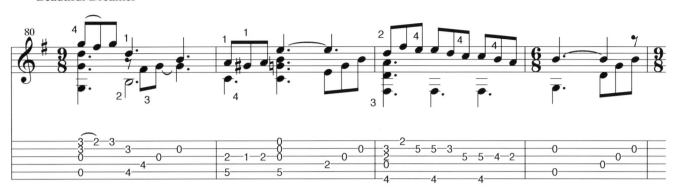

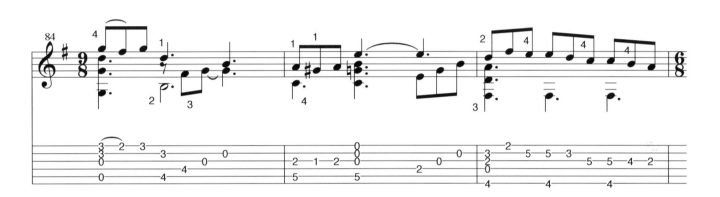

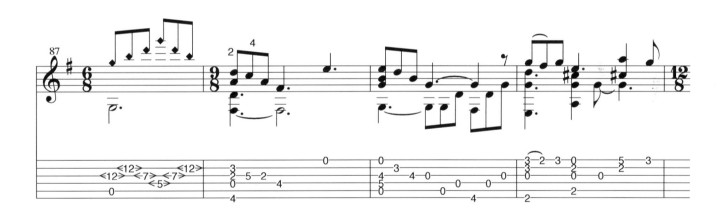

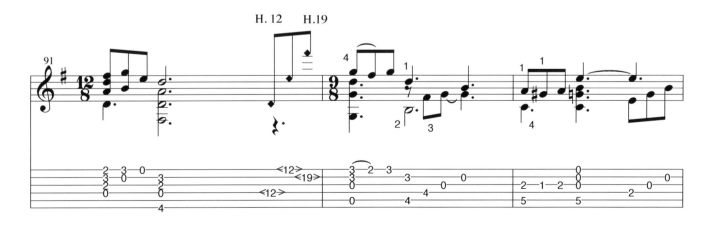

Old Folks at Home
(Swanee)

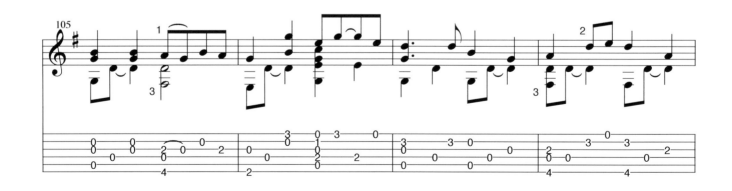

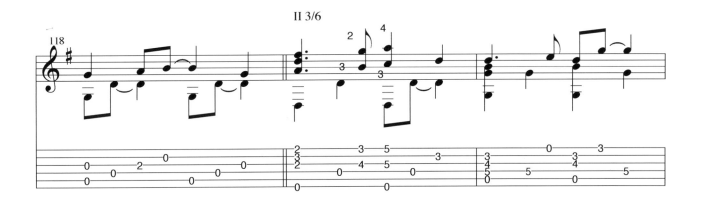

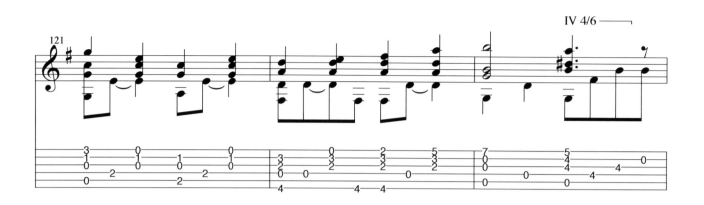

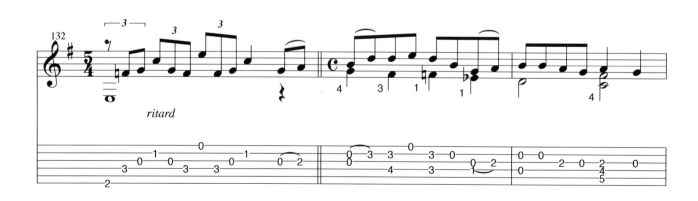

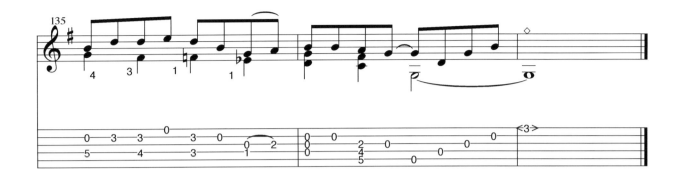

Simple Gifts

6 = D
5 = G

Capo 3

Tambour

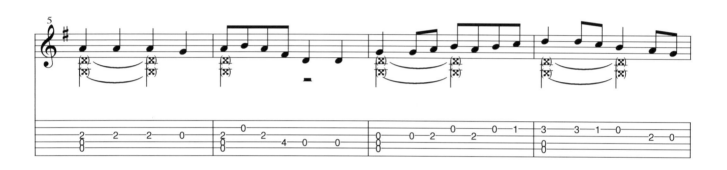

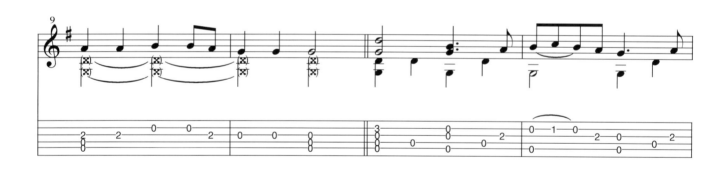

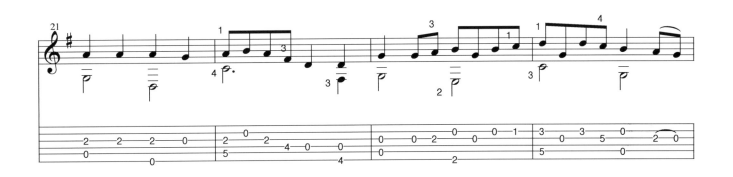

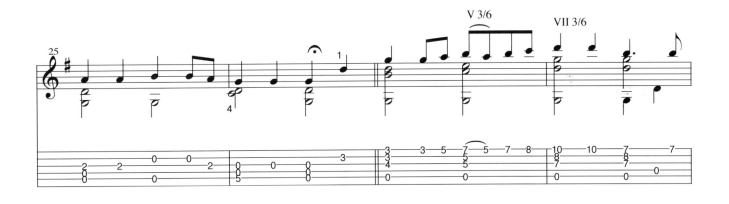

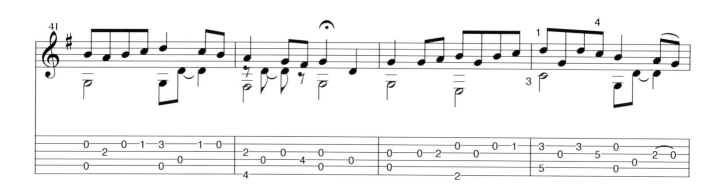

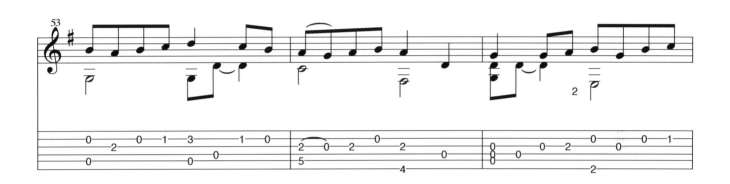

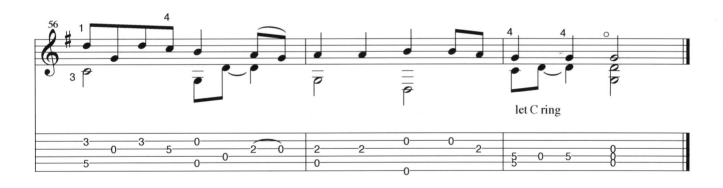

Deep River

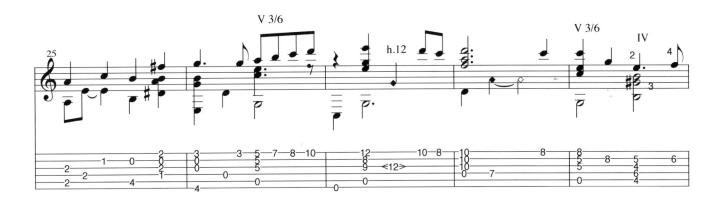
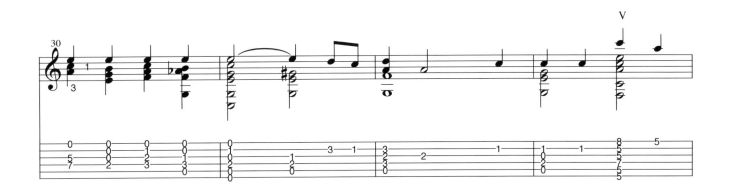

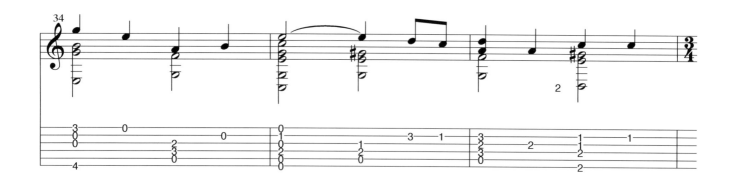

Bound for the Promised Land

Capo VI

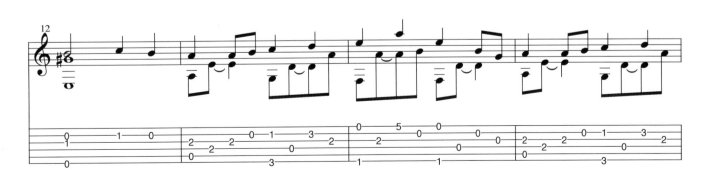

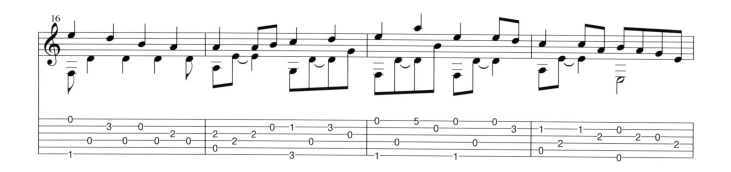

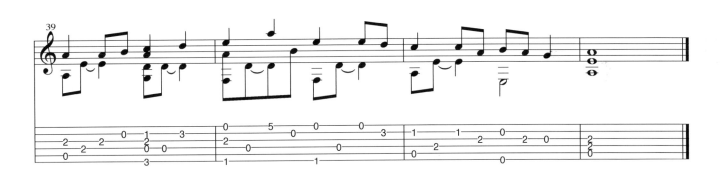

The Water Is Wide

6 = C
5 = G

Fifteen Years on the Erie Canal

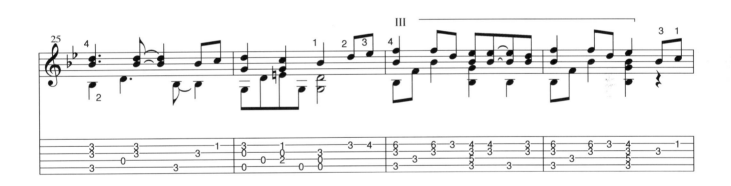

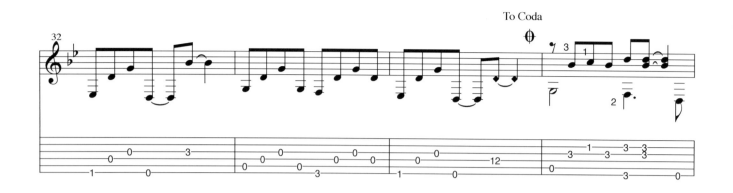

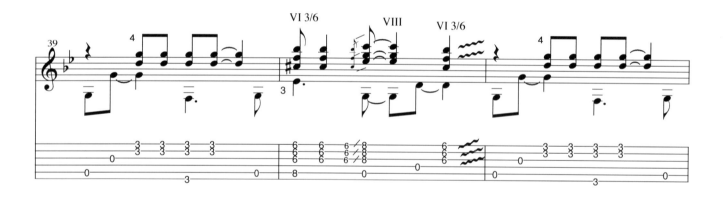

D.S. al Coda

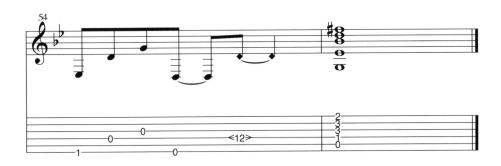

81

Frontier Medley

6 = D
Capo II

Home On The Range

III 3/6

Red River Valley

She'll Be Comin' 'Round The Mountain

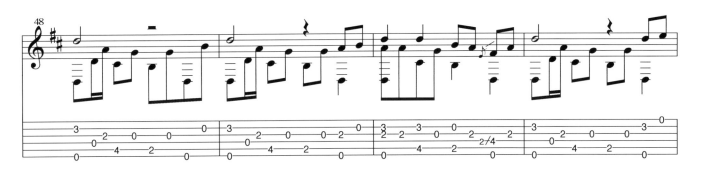

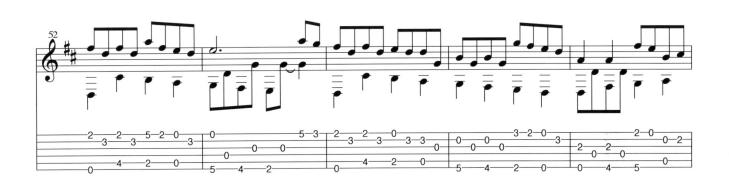

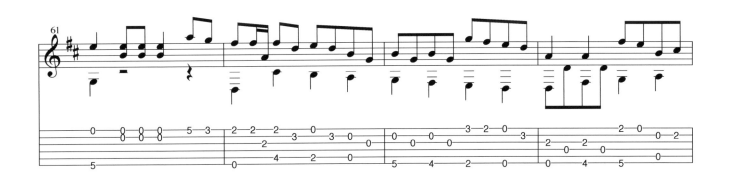

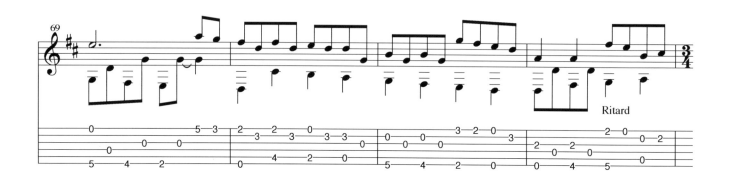

Break time, much slower

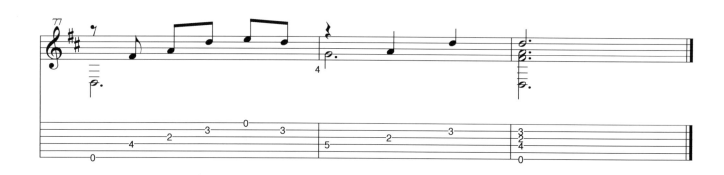

Aura Lee

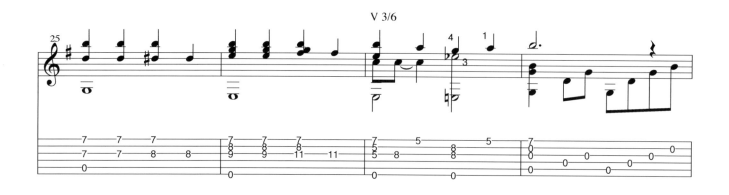

89

Civil War Medley

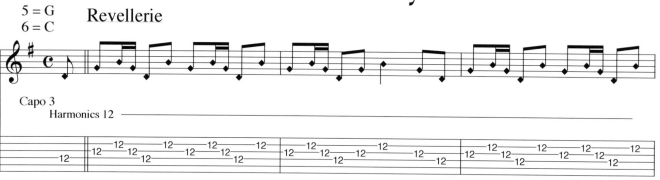

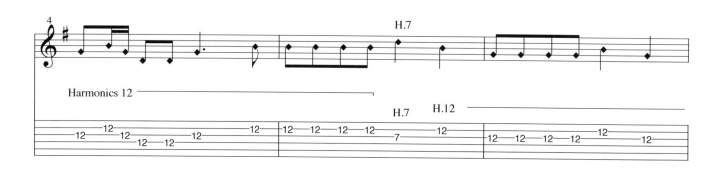

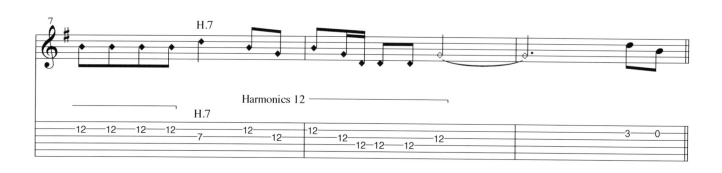

Dixie

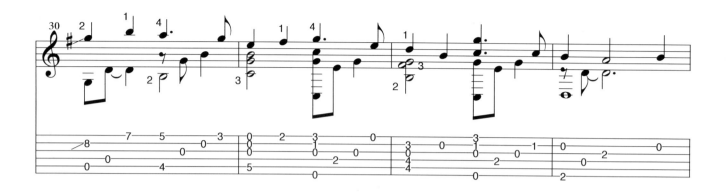

Battle Cry of Freedom

Bonnie Blue Flag

Tap the bridge

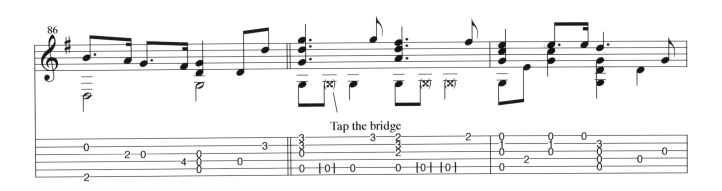

Lincoln and Liberty

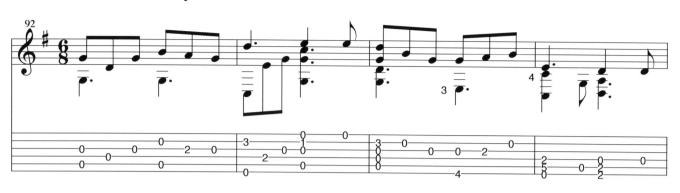

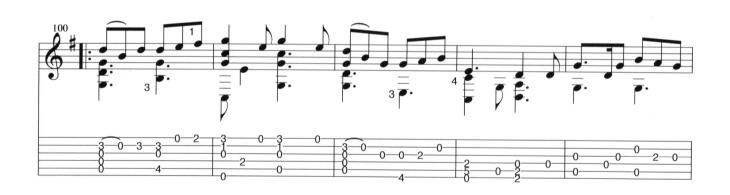

96

All Quiet Along the Potomac Tonight

Tenting Tonight on the Old Camp Ground

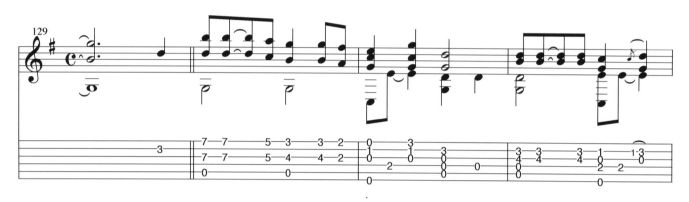

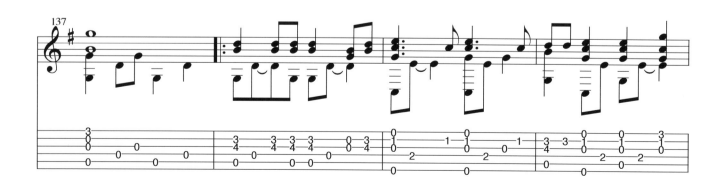

Taps

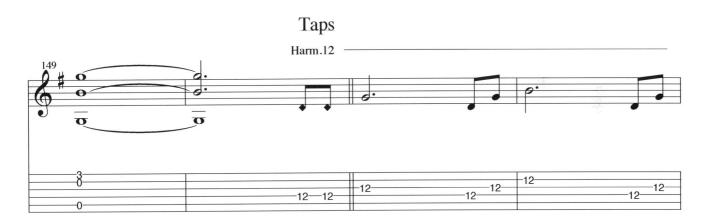

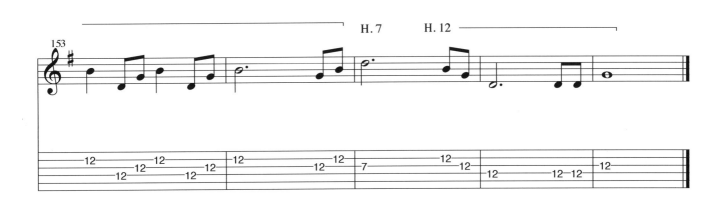

When Johnny Comes Marching Home

6 = C Capo III
5 = G Muted Bass

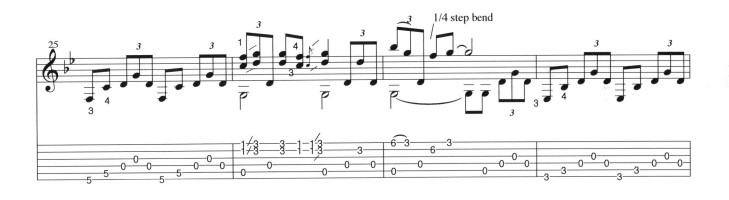

101

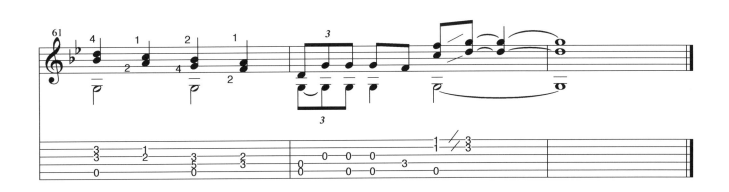

6 = D
5 = G

Armed Services Medley

The Caissons Go Rolling Along

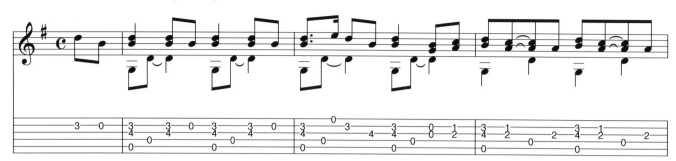

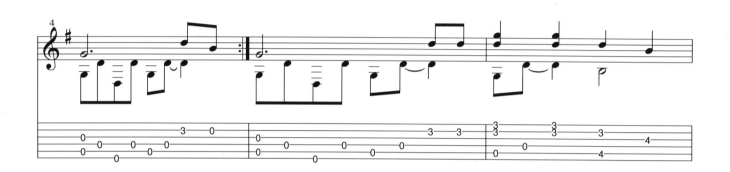

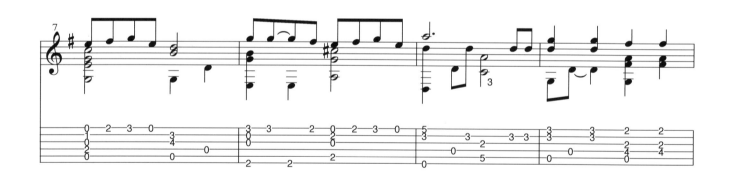

The U.S. Air Force - (Wild Blue Yonder)

Anchors Aweigh

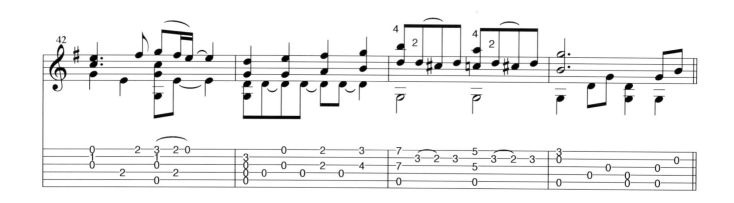

From the Halls of Montezuma

Mutted Bass

P

Long Fade and Ritard

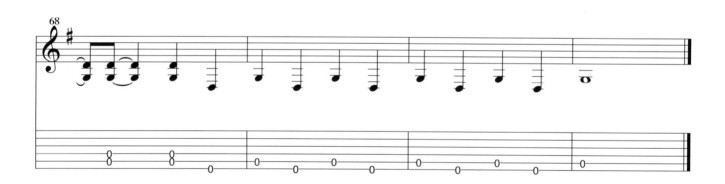

America the Beautiful

6 = D
5 = G

110

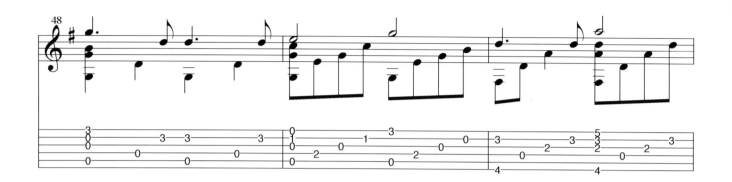

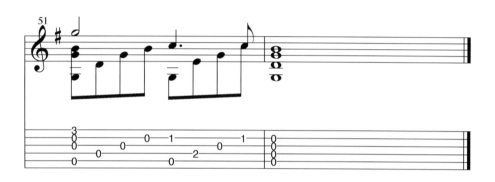

Capo IV

The Battle Hymn of the Republic

6 = D
5 = G

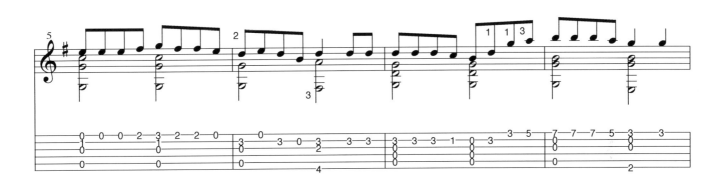

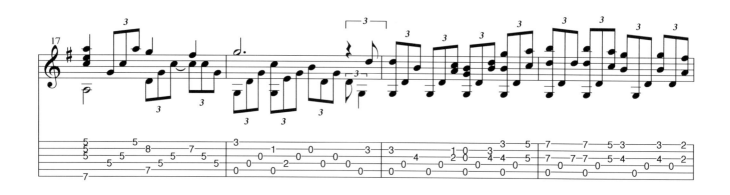

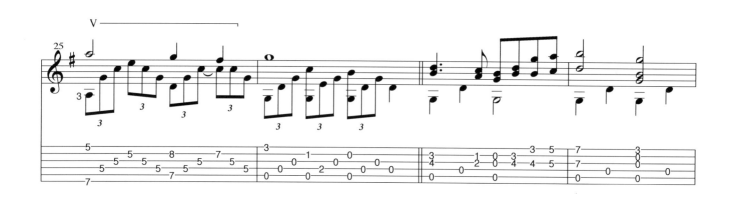

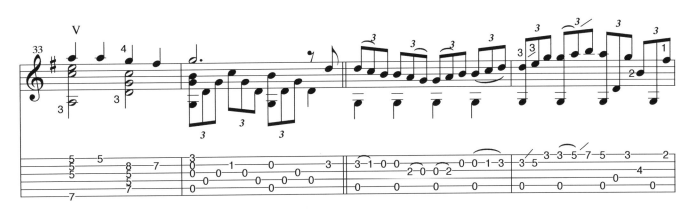

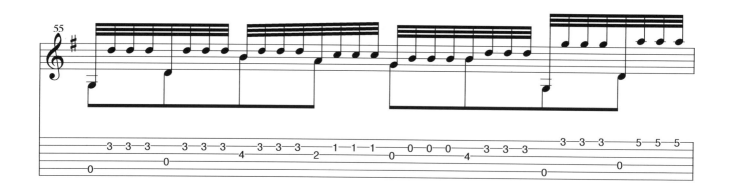

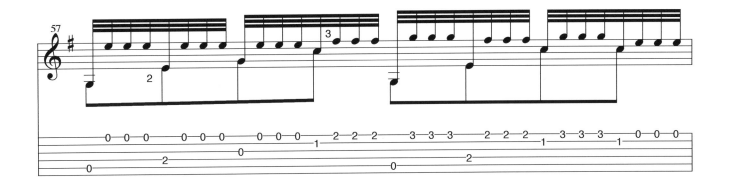

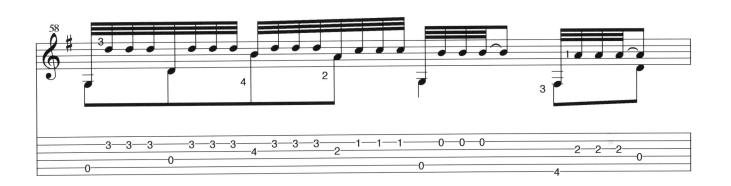

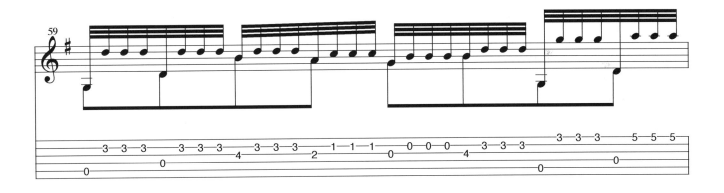

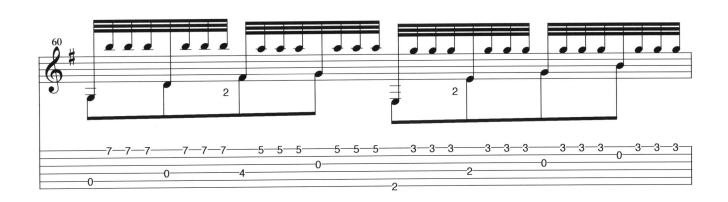

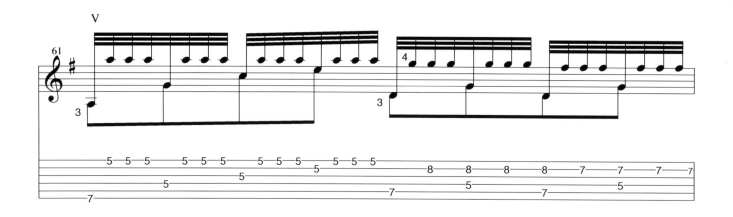

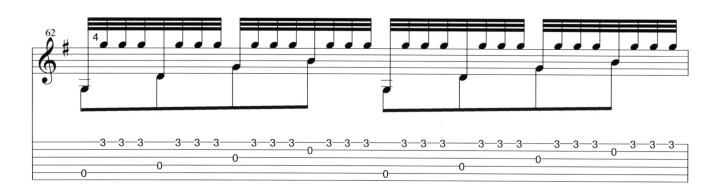

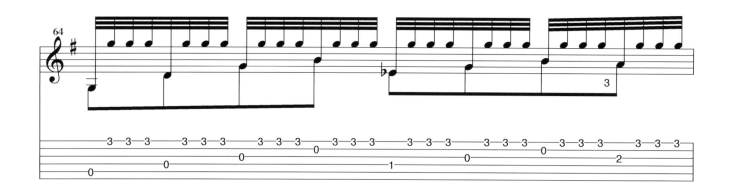

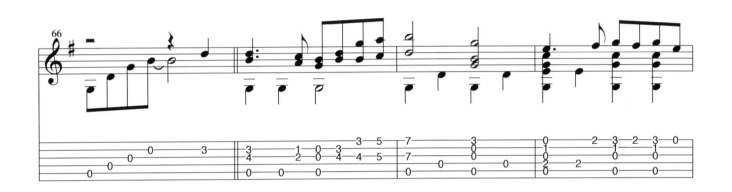

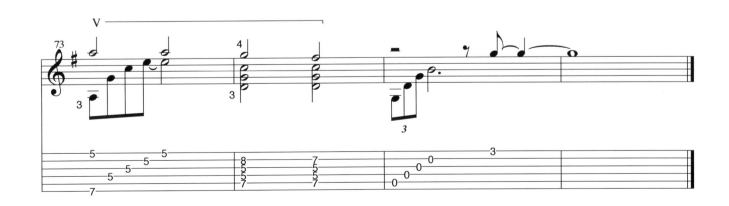

The history behind the making of American Treasures
(An excerpt from the American Treasures CD liner notes - used with permission)

One of the many wondrous effects of music is the way it can connect us to history. I hope the historical notes along with these solo guitar arrangements will provide a refreshing remembrance of our past. Perhaps, putting the pieces of our history together in this way will also stir a deeper appreciation for this country and for those whose faith, devotion, and hard work helped to establish it as a great nation.

The idea of assembling a collection of American patriotic melodies on classical guitar began when I lived in Boston back in 1991. While watching a news broadcast on the Persian Gulf War, the sight of American troops leaving home to protect another country began to stir my own feelings of patriotism. I began to arrange some traditional patriotic classics with the goal of recapturing, instrumentally, the spirit of the compositions. Around that same time a friend gave me a book entitled *The Rebirth of America*, an intriguing account of the spiritual roots behind the birth of our country. I soon realized how much I had taken for granted, namely, the price paid by the forefathers for the freedoms I enjoy as an American citizen. It's so easy to forget that when the Declaration of Independence was presented to Congress on August 2, 1776 for signatures, most of the 56 men who put their name to the document did so fully realizing the dangerous consequences of their actions. To sign a document that publicly accused King George of "repeated injuries and usurpations," and to announce that Americans were therefore "absolved from all allegiance to the British Crown," was going to be considered an act of treason. They knew they were risking their fortunes and that possible execution was up ahead.

"For the support of this declaration, with a firm reliance on the
protection of Divine Providence, we mutually pledge to each other our lives, our fortunes and our sacred honor."
-- The signers of the Declaration of Independence

Freedom is never free; it is purchased at great cost. The men who drafted and signed the Declaration of Independence were not just using eloquent words but were courageously taking a united stand to pay freedom's price.

"Posterity - you will never know how much it has cost my generation to preserve your freedom. I hope you make good use of it."
-- John Quincy Adams

They were rich, well-educated men who enjoyed much ease and luxury in their personal lives. Many were wealthy landowners. In order to give their time and effort to establish their country's liberty, they all had to give up their own private businesses. They let their properties and estates deteriorate while away from home and risked complete destruction of their homes by the British. They became the target for British retaliation and suffered great losses. Twelve had their homes from Rhode Island to Charleston sacked, looted, occupied by the enemy, or burned. The British ravaged their estates, destroyed vast woodlands, butchered their cattle, and sent their families fleeing for their lives. Robert Stockton of New Jersey, for example, was captured and brutally mistreated. He was exposed to bitter cold and then placed in prison. His beautiful estate near Princeton had been used as a military headquarters by the British who destroyed his library, furniture, and his writings. Francis Lewis not only had his home and properties destroyed, but the British jailed his wife, injuring her health which hastened her death. John Hart, who was 65 years old when he signed the Declaration of Independence, was driven from his wife's bedside as she lay dying. Their children fled for their lives. For more than a year, he lived in forests and caves returning home to find his wife dead. Upon finding his farm completely destroyed and with no hope of rebuilding his fortune, his health failed and he died from exhaustion. Thomas Nelson Jr. raised two million dollars for the patriots' cause on his own personal credit. The government never compensated him, and repaying the loans wiped out his entire estate. Nelson spent his fortune for his country and yet was buried in an unmarked grave. Such were some of the sacrifices of the American Revolution. These 56 men considered liberty more important than the security they enjoyed. They paid the price in order to obtain freedom. We are in their debt to this day.

May this music and the retelling of this history help to keep the memory of their faith, courage, and personal sacrifices ever before us.

Our history is truly amazing. The United States has passed more social legislation and enacted more laws promoting individual liberty than any other nation in world history. Although we are only 225 years old as a nation, countries around the world look with awe at our freedoms, our treasures. To what shall we attribute the secret of our progress? The following quotations point to something often overlooked -- our spiritual heritage. One of Washington's early official acts as President was establishing the *Thanksgiving Proclamation* which reads:
"Whereas it is the duty of all nations to acknowledge the providence of Almighty God, to obey His will, to be grateful for
His benefits and humbly implore His protection and favor."
-- President George Washington

"The moral principles and precepts contained in the Scriptures ought to form the basis of all our civil constitutions and laws..."
-- Noah Webster

We as a nation, however, have been moving farther away from these principles that gave us the basis for our freedoms. Lincoln said it best on April 30, 1863:
"We have been the recipients of the choicest bounties of heaven. We have been preserved, these many years, in peace and prosperity. We
have grown in numbers, wealth and power, as no other nation has ever grown. But we have forgotten God. We have forgotten the gracious
hand which preserved us in peace, and multiplied and enriched and strengthened us; and we have vainly imagined, in the deceitfulness of
our hearts, that all these blessings were produced by some superior wisdom and virtue of our own. Intoxicated with unbroken success, we
have become too self-sufficient to feel the necessity of redeeming and preserving grace, too proud to pray to the God that made us! It
behooves us, then, to humble ourselves before the offended Power, to confess our national sins,
and to pray for clemency and forgiveness."
-- President Abraham Lincoln

Romans 1:18-32 in the New Testament describes the social patterns that resulted in the collapse of the powerful Roman empire. Those same patterns are appearing in our country today, threatening to erode families and the values upon which our country was built. As in the days of our founding fathers, men and women with deep convictions and courage must take a stand for what is morally and spiritually right in order to preserve our most valuable American Treasures.

"My God! how little do my countrymen know what precious blessings they are in
possession of, and which no other people on earth enjoy."
--Thomas Jefferson

American Treasures features extensive program liner notes on the history of all the selections on the recording. The American Treasures CD can be ordered on the web at www.cdbaby.com/lestermusic3.

More information is available at the artist's website at www.GuitarArtistry.com

Made in the USA
Middletown, DE
15 April 2015